# Air Guitar: Art
# Reconsidering
# Rock Music

CW00421914

curated by Emma Mahony

# Contents

**Foreword**  Music can make a mark in people's lives, it can be a point of crisis within society or the soft glow of a loving memory. We all remember the act of our first purchase, our private motivation becoming public through an act of monetary exchange. *Air Guitar: Art Reconsidering Rock Music* explores the relationship between contemporary art and rock music from the perspective of the artist as music fan. The exhibition examines how music from the '70s, '80s and '90s has influenced a generation of visual artists. As glam rock and progressive rock were reaching their climax, as evidenced by Queen's *Bohemian Rhapsody* selling 2.1 million copies, making it the third best-selling single of all time, its camp melodrama was followed by the 'back to basics' attitude of punk. Punk came out of boredom, insecurity, the longing for something to change, much of the same motivation for artists who question the world in which we live. Some of those artists use rock music as a source of inspiration and inevitably it demands a look over their shoulder. The teenage bedroom – we have all been there – is the set for cult followings of almost religious intensity, the hedonism of youth culture or a place of imagined miserabilism. Our favourites will range from syrupy love songs to angst-ridden tirades and from introspective tunes to stadium anthems. *Air Guitar* brings us back to our bedrooms, to our own relationship between music and our lives. Music is an element of cultural expression, as is contemporary art. Bringing them together is to create an opportunity for new audiences to engage with something that is close to their hearts and to share that experience.

We would like to thank Emma Mahony who has curated *Air Guitar* for bringing together work by emerging and well-established artists. *Air Guitar* will tour to Cornerhouse, Manchester, Angel Row, Nottingham, Tullie House, Carlisle and has been supported by the National Touring Programme funded by the Arts Council of England. A list of people we wish to acknowledge is on page 72 and above all we would like to thank the artists for working closely with us on the exhibition and the catalogue.

**Stephen Snoddy**
Director

**Elisabetta Fabrizi**
Exhibitions Organiser

And if the world does turn
and if London burns,
i'll be standing on the beach
with my guitar.
i want to be in a band
when i get to heaven,
anyone can play guitar
and they won't be a nothing
any more.

The relationship between the insular art world and the ubiquitous world of rock is a long and curious one. On the one hand, there are those artists who dabble, forging the path from art school to rock stardom. In Britain The Jam acknowledged such a legacy by titling their 1977 hit *Art School*. In the US, David Byrne of Talking Heads met his fellow band members at Rhode Island School of Design and his first band was aptly titled The Artistics. Freddie Mercury painted pop stars when studying at Ealing College of Art and Malcolm McLaren persuaded Sex Pistols' bassist Glen Matlock to enroll for a foundation course at St Martins so that he would not have to miss any rehearsals to 'sign on'. Not to forget the countless other music personalities who studied at art school, a list that is a role call of rock celebrities. Traffic flows both ways though, not only have art students graduated to rock stardom, rock music has provided an enduring frame of reference for a generation of visual artists.

In an extremely catholic music scene, rock appears to have an unreasonably strong conceptual hold over visual artists, considering that it has long since been displaced by pop in all its multifarious forms. Perhaps, as Matthew Slotover suggests: '[rock music] still carries connotations of rebellion and nonconformism. Some artists are still attracted to that kind of glamour.' Music is just part of the bigger picture that infiltrates the artist's approach: the myths, fictions, seminal moments and casualties of rock's excesses are all part of the territory explored by this exhibition.

Matthew Slotover, quoted in Alix Sharkey, *Artful Rockers*, 'ES Magazine', 6 August 1999

For many of the artists exhibiting in *Air Guitar*, rock music is a constant source of inspiration, for others it is a subtle influence. Their vantage point is a genuine one, coming as it does from the perspective of a fan. It is a perspective which demands a timely and unapologetic glance backwards to the aspirations and suburban angst of the adolescent, back to the legacy of the teenage bedroom. One-time allegiances and passions are revisited; the air guitar is unearthed and dusted down.

*Air Guitar* examines the production of rock-inspired art made at the end of the twentieth century by a generation of artists whose earliest memories are of the '60s and the first part of the '70s. Their retrospective take is rooted in the '60s of The Rolling Stones and moves quickly on to embrace the '70s punk scene of The Sex Pistols and The Clash via Bowie and glam rock. The trajectory continues through the late '70s and early '80s of Joy Division and The Fall, the cutoff point being Nirvana's grundge movement, which resurrected punk in the early '90s.

Scott King and Sam Durant assume the guise of analysts of popular culture, investigating the ideals of the '60s and '70s and how they have collapsed and gone awry. They look to seminal moments in the rollercoaster history of rock for inspiration, moments which often parallel other noteworthy historical and cultural events, such as the Altamont tragedy and the 'live fast, die young' school of thought. Unable to play at Woodstock in 1969, The Rolling Stones staged their own version of the 'free concert' on the West Coast of America in the same year. Held at Altamont Raceway in Tracey, California, the Altamont concert is seen by many cultural commentators, Durant included, as the single moment which signalled the downfall of the '60s. Rather than revisiting the hippie utopia that was associated with Woodstock, Altamont disintegrated

Non-Site, Scatological *Disaster* Dead
Have some Sympathy

into a distopia when the Hell's Angels hired to keep the peace began beating up the revel-ers. The musicians did not escape their wrath either; during a set by Jefferson Airplane the lead singer Marty Balin was knocked unconscious in an on-stage brawl. The chaos was such that The Grateful Dead, fearful for their lives, backed out at the last minute. Ignoring Mick Jagger's earnest pleas to keep the peace, the concert reached its fateful finale when Meredith Hunter, a gun-wielding concertgoer, was stabbed to death by a Hell's Angel during a rendition of *Under My Thumb* by The Rolling Stones. There were three other casualties at Altamont that day, two were run over and a third was killed when he jumped off an aqueduct whilst high on LSD.

The mantra 'live fast, die young' has been fatally embraced by many of the icons of rock from Jimi Hendrix to Keith Moon. It was even borrowed by Kurt Cobain in the wording of his suicide note 'it's better to burn out than fade away'. Taking this 'death culture' as his starting point, Scott King has translated the often unglamorous and tragic reality of rock suicides into a statistical analysis. *Into the Black*, 1999 (the title is borrowed from Neil Young's *Hey Hey, My My, Into the Black*), a series of digitally authored pie charts which mimic corporate marketing strategies, delineates the similarly tragic fates of Ian Curtis of Joy Division, Kurt Cobain of Nirvana and Manic Street Preachers' guitarist Richey Edwards. In a consciously irreverent and clinical rendering King breaks down their careers into four simplistic but pivotal stages, each occupying one of the four intercon-necting circles on the chart. They all wrote songs about pain and now they are all dead, each tormented by their personal demons. Cobain blew his head off with a shotgun,

Ian Curtis hung himself in his kitchen and Richey Edwards mysteriously disappeared in 1995 and has not been seen since, although rumours of sightings are rife. By reducing their multi-coloured lives to black and white statistics, King questions the gritty reality behind the mythologised facade of the record industry.

Similarly, the Los Angeles artist Sam Durant utilises diagrammatic analysis to draw links from the high art practices of post-minimalism to the mass mediated popular culture industry. His *Quaternary Field Associative Diagram*, 1998, an appropriated version of an earlier diagram by Rosalind Krauss from her 1978 essay *Sculpture in the Expanded Field*, perfectly sets the scene. Employing the same system of horizontals, verticals and intersections used by Krauss to order modernist sculpture, Durant traces links from Robert Smithson's *Partially Buried Woodshed* to Altamont, The Rolling Stones, Neil Young and Kurt Cobain. The route he takes is via the persona of a pop star, a song lyric, urban legends and modernist theory. Entropy, in all its cultural and artistic guises, is the glue which gels these seemingly unrelated events together.

Not unlike in King's work, death plays a large part in Durant's practice and it appears to be the key to his circular logic. From Smithson's early death in a plane crash (like a rock star in his prime) to the untimely suicide of Cobain (a rock star in his prime), coupled with the Altamont tragedy and the killings at Kent State, Durant's logic comes full circle to represent the meltdown of the '60s. Born one generation too late to have partied at Woodstock, rioted at Altamont or protested at Kent State, Durant and King are informed by an analysis of history as impartial as its nature will allow. Their intention is not to

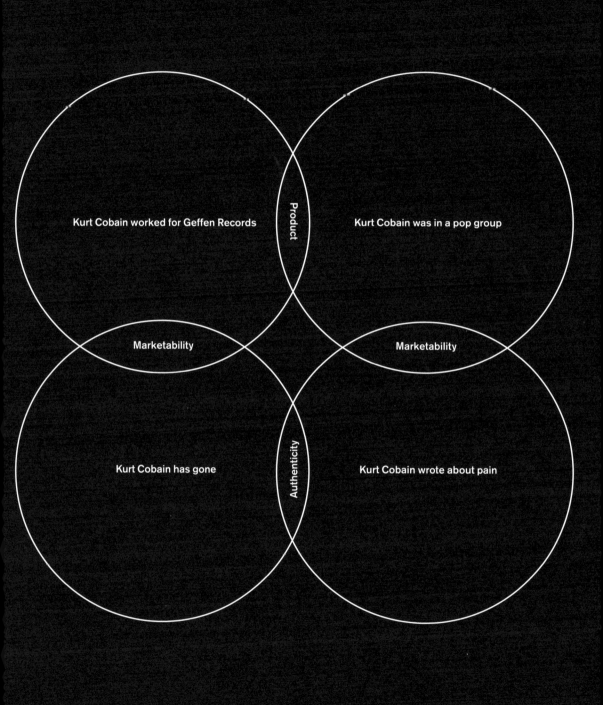

Kurt cobain was born NEAR seattle

he was the guitarist and singer  in the pop group nirvana

They made SONGS ABOUT DESPAIR

these were pressed onto a variety of plastics and sold around the world

on 5 april 1994 cobain took a shoTgun and blew his own head off

AT HOME in seattle

swallow the romantic cliché whole, but slowly to chip away at the myth created by the music industry and gradually to reveal its less than glamorous core.

Stephen Willats belongs to an older generation than that of most of the artists in *Air Guitar* and experienced first-hand those seminal moments that Durant, King and others rely on history to recount. The social research which informs his practice has always been greatly influenced by his long standing interest in music, in particular punk. In the late '70s Willats frequented the Roxy Club in Covent Garden, a short-lived underground punk venue, where bands such as The Sex Pistols, The Dammed, Screwdriver and The Drones debuted. He also avidly collected limited edition cassette recordings and 45rpm DIY singles produced by punk groups. This experience was the catalyst for *Into the Night*, a series of works which tells the multi-faceted story of the punk movement, how its DIY ethos effected the rise of new social groupings bound as much by aesthetic and social values as by musical taste. Introduced to what he terms 'the world of the night' in 1981 by a chance meeting with an ex-student, Willats attended the numerous makeshift clubs which were springing up around London and befriended the groups who congregated there. *Into the Night* reflects the five years he spent clubbing by night and sleeping by day, interviewing the clubs organisers and members and making documentary-based work in response to their beliefs and value systems. 'The night has always been a very potent territory for groups to define themselves as a capsule, to conceal themselves from the prying eyes of dominant culture.' Stephen Willats, *Living like a Goya*, in 'Means of Escape' (Exh. cat.), Rochdale Art Gallery, 1983

Taking a less analytical and more nostalgic stance than Durant, King and Willats, there

are other artists in *Air Guitar* who mine the pop cultural heritage of their youth for inspiration. Their work is perhaps more accessible to some subcultural groups than others.
Certainly, an in-depth level of music knowledge is a prerequisite to a full understanding
of their work. They are those rock aficionados who, for the purpose of this essay are
termed 'bedroom fans'.

In his novel *American Psycho*, Brett Easton Ellis's protagonist Patrick Bateman
(a.k.a. the American Psycho) exhibits traits of the 'bedroom fan' when he subjects his
victims to extremely self-indulgent and painfully boring monologues on his '80s music
interests. Entire chapters are devoted to his musings on Genesis, Whitney Houston and
Huey Lewis and The News. Maike Abetz & Oliver Drescher, Paul Housley, Paul McDevitt,
James Pyman, George Shaw and Michael Wilkinson could perhaps be described as closet
'bedroom fans'. They are only too keen to divulge their encyclopaedic knowledge of rock
music to any available ear whether, like Bateman's intended victims, they are listening
or just pretending to be. They approach the process of making art with the same
anorak determination they allocate to music; the fastidiousness of an adolescent youth
comes to mind.

To the initiated, the patchwork of album covers that forms the backdrop of Maike
Abetz & Oliver Drescher's paintings is heavily laden with art and rock references and
tells us of a complex iconography. Theirs is a world where an icon of soul such as Chris
Mayfield is juxtaposed with Public Enemy and Kraftwerk; where the androgynous looking
young men and women who populate the canvases recall the gender-bending which

became part and parcel of the spectacle that was the '70s glam rock music industry, while simultaneously looking very contemporary.

Similarly, Michael Wilkinson leafs through the shelves of record stores to feed his passion for the graphic qualities of '80s vinyl. Taking the record sleeves from his personal record collection as the starting point for his paintings, he removes all visual signifiers leaving pared down areas of flat colour. Stripped of text and images, the resulting 12 x 12 inch square paintings have their original form concealed to all but those who own the same edition. In his simulation of Kraftwerk's *Autobahn,* the title of the album and the band's name have been edited out until the painting's reference is unrecognizable to all but those familiar with the album's graphic symbol of a road receding into the distance. Other examples are more obscure in their reference to the originals. The Smiths' *Hatful of Hollow* has been condensed to its blue and white background and Joy Division's album *Closer* has been radically pared down to all but a fine black line that runs around the sleeves edge.

James Pyman's intricately rendered pencil drawings recall a time when drawing skills were highly desirable, when it was considered cool to graffiti your copybooks and school desks with the names of your favourite rock stars whether out of boredom, protest or obsession. Any of these three states of mind may have induced the minor act of childhood vandalism evident in Pyman's pencil drawing *1979*, 1996. Close inspection of the school desk centered in the foreground of the picture reveals a heart crudely carved into its surface within which the first names of the members of Joy Division – Ian, Brian, Pete and Steve – are scratched. The names, together with the date which titles the drawing, make the work all the more poignant. Frances Stark on the other hand could perhaps be described as the wiser, more mature descendent of those teenagers who emblazoned their copybooks with the logos and song lyrics of their idols. In her own words, the implication of being a groupie is 'some sort of mutant nihilistic sentimentalisation of the anti-hero.' Stark's method of drawing recalls punk's embrace of trial and error, the stuff of amateurism. She painstakingly transcribes blocks of text from literary and musical sources using carbon paper. In the resulting works, words are often split apart and written horizontally, the letters isolated on the page. A horizontal repetition of the lyrics 'fitter, happier' taken from Radiohead's *OK Computer* album is the basis for *more productive (from Radiohead: OK Computer)*, 1998.

To conclude with the topic of Radiohead, on their album *Pablo Honey* they released the rather aspirational *Anyone can play guitar*. What the song omitted to say is that not everyone can play guitar very well. However, this is not really the point. The self-confessed musical amateurism of many of the artists in this exhibition allows them to sidestep the scrutiny of the music industry. They are content to incorporate music and performance into their work as a means to extend their art practices conceptually. While it is important to say that theirs is not a nostalgic revisiting of rock's past, for many of the artists in *Air Guitar* their past musical interests will always remain clearly in their sights. It is almost as if they and their onetime musical allegiances were frozen forever in a mosh-pit moment in time.

The room is packed. Crammed into one corner is a drumkit, amplifiers and rudimentary PA system, through which the young singer shouts and snarls his way through six punk-pop guitar numbers. It's hot and the walls are sweating.

The room is packed. Crammed into one corner is a drumkit, amplifiers and rudimentary PA system, through which the young singer shouts and snarls his way through six punk-pop guitar numbers. It's hot and the walls are sweating. At the end we all cheer and clap but I haven't been engaged with the music as I would be at a normal gig. Instead I've been thinking how clever the conceit is. Because this is an art project by Dale Holmes and Dave Webb, the simulacrum of a tribute band, paying homage to a bunch of punk-pop brats who made a small splash in the music scene back in the late '80s. Back then, in the shadow of rave and hip-hop, everyone wanted to know how rock music could survive and for bands like Semloh Bbew, looking back to The Stooges seemed like a way forward. Except that the original Semloh Bbew didn't actually exist. The musicians in front of me are playing the role of tribute act, paying homage to an imaginary outfit, themselves supposedly fixated on earlier precedents. The layers recede, the beer flows, the audience inspects the silk-screened T-shirts and posters pinned up around the room and it all seems to fit together. If this seems like a successful art project then it's an indication of the ease with which supposedly highbrow contemporary art now colonises pop culture. Both art and music have converged on the cult of personality and the entertainment industry, each paradox-ically in search of a sense of authenticity and validation in the eyes of the other.

British artists have entered the tabloid arena on the same level as the latest pop idol, and Groucho Club culture reigns supreme, but this is just the most recent manifestation of a relationship that goes back decades. Jackson Pollock's wild gestural abstraction is forever linked to the sound of free jazz and it is impossible to think of Andy Warhol without hearing the music of The Velvet Underground and Nico, Patti Smith and Robert Mapplethorpe, Basquiat and the New York street scene, right up to today's proliferation of artist's bands including Low Expectations, Interspecies Lovechild and Turner Prize-winner Martin Creed's outfit Owada. It seems that the music world offers something that artists want beyond the immediate pleasures of glamour and mass-market appeal.

It works the other way around as well. When Don van Vliet, better known as Captain Beefheart, gave up making music for painting in 1983, he was returning to his first love (between the ages of 5 and 13 Beefheart had a weekly slot on television displaying clay animal sculptures) and quickly found champions in Julian Schnabel and gallerist Mary Boone. It seems that making a series of seminal underground albums including the legendary *Trout Mask Replica* wasn't enough for him. The same could be said of other star names including John Lennon and Paul McCartney, Miles Davis, Jerry Garcia, David Bowie and Brian Eno. There is something that seems to attract musicians at a certain stage of their career, once they have done with the throwaway appeal of pop music. Rock'n'roll is only now really starting to grow up and look back at itself, witness the success of adult monthlies like *Q* and a burgeoning tide of heavyweight analytical hardbacks on the shelves of high street retailers. Art, on the other hand, has never suffered from a lack of seriousness, it can be, always has been, a way to acquire a particular kind of social status. Listening to *Lucky Star* back in 1983, who would have foreseen Madonna as vice-president of the ICA in London or lending Frida Kahlo paintings to Tate Modern?

Offering freedom and a community of like-minded souls for the terminally alienated,

Photo from the Semloh Bbew
Fanclub meeting at the Dragon Bar,
East London, 30 October 2001

art schools have long provided a stopping off point on the way to the rehearsal room for aspiring musicians. The broad creative education encourages students to develop their own interests as much as their drawing skills and turns out thousands of individuals destined to be singers, guitarists and drummers alongside the designers and fine artists perhaps more hoped-for by their tutors. But more than that, the freedom and license permits a certain bohemianism that has always been attractive. Think of Mick Jagger as a classic Romantic icon, representing radical self-determination in the face of a bourgeois society. When rock stars need a role model they turn to the myth of the artist, when they get too caught up in the wheels of the music industry it makes sense that they should turn to art, emblematic of pure expressionism, as their release.

Record companies have their own commercial agenda which often rubs up against the desires of their pampered stars. Some albums sit on the shelf for years awaiting release, so that marketing departments can be geared up and financial issues carefully negotiated. When they eventually do appear in the shops a round of promotional duties and touring follows, which might be dragged out for years as each global territory is methodically worked through in turn. That doesn't allow much room for spontaneity. Even within the dynamics of a band the creative process is constantly subject to pragmatism, individual tastes often being submerged below the demands of musicians' egos, produc- ers' advice and studio budgets. No wonder so many musicians crave the freedom and the unfettered individuality that artists represent.

So it is ironic that for at least three generations of artists, the whole idea of pure

Photo from the Semloh Bbew
Fanclub meeting at the Dragon Bar,
East London, 30 October 2001

expression and unbridled subjectivity has been shattered by a philosophy that declares the author dead, and no one more than the sum of their cultural influences. When contemporary artists reach out to rock music in return, they are most often reaching out to that part of it which is still thought of as authentic. The totemic autonomy of the singer-songwriter — one man and his guitar — that is the modern day parallel to the bohemian ideal that inspired so many musicians. At its peak, during the '70s in America, much of the music being made was additionally underpinned by ideas of the land and a connection to national history. The Band, The Grateful Dead and most of all Neil Young, played with the idea that today's sound might draw inspiration from the music of the past whether that be the blues or the folk of Appalachian mountain trails. To hear the growl of a voice over hanging chords or the rush of exhilaration as the drums kicked in was to invoke a memory of an earlier place and time. The success of these artists had the effect of framing the experience of generations of music fans in a kind of golden glow. Rock music tapped into traditions of songwriting and storytelling that went back centuries, and you could feel it. When at times it has attempted to push forward, to become 'arty', it has also inevitably become something else: progressive rock, jazz-rock, post-rock. Always something other, as if rock as a category were too inflexible to allow any deviation from the norm. It is this clear sense of identity and deep-rooted history that exerts a powerful pull to contemporary artists who are almost defined by their loss of connection to reality.

Looking back at earlier decades, today's artists understand the stars of this golden age as mythical figures rather than individuals, and to a certain extent musicians have willingly undertaken these archetypal roles in exchange for the communicative power that they command. They have become the history which culture draws upon to narrate itself, the vocabulary of possible meanings. The dangerous curse of success might be represented by Michael Jackson, now a figure of pity rather than awe, while Bono might stand for the virtue of old fashioned hard graft. Madonna has many myths, but above all transformation and growth, while Kurt Cobain and Jim Morrison must represent the perils of poetic oversensitivity. Elvis is the biggest of them all, naturally. A Christ-like figure living in Graceland, in his life he overtly drew on the iconography of the Sun gods. In death the myth plays out in a proliferation of sightings that continues to this day.

In seeking to engage with these stories, or to appropriate a little of the heroic authenticity that rock stars possess, contemporary artists are consciously drawing on a rich store of shared experience. Everyone has a favourite song, after all, and can anyone really claim not to have looked up at a poster on their bedroom wall and wished themselves away? Even the most serious minded conceptual artist was a teenager once. Returning to those feelings from an adult perspective permits a certain distancing, naive sentiment reframed as an outsider art stance. Amongst the proliferation of sub-genres thrown up by each generation's urgent need to have something of its own rock music has been a constant presence. The White Stripes, The Pixies, Sonic Youth, Nirvana ... names and haircuts change but the attitude is immediately recognisable, the still point in a hyperactive market-driven scene. A visceral thrill, an electric charge. Three chords, six strings and one voice against the world.

# Maike Abetz & Oliver Drescher

Born Dusseldorf, 1970 and Essen, 1969. They live and work in Berlin.

*Radiowellen*, 2000
Acrylic on canvas
180 x 240 cm
Courtesy arsFutura Galerie, Zurich

The world depicted in Maike Abetz & Oliver Drescher's paintings combines elements of dreams and stardom, music and TV, the things that occupy us in private moments. Amid a sea of references, the characters in their paintings are ambiguous leaving us to question if they are portraits of everyday people or famous musicians such as Iggy Pop, David Bowie or Jimi Hendrix.

The environment in which the subjects of their works play records, air guitar and spray graffiti suggests a fantasy world fuelled by media images. From record covers to DNA chains, from Mandelbrot patterns to Op Art designs, there is a sense of cultural 'cross-over' where image and meaning are combined into hybrid forms. Since Elvis, sexuality, charisma and performance took their place alongside the music as the defining elements in the success of a band or a performer, but it isn't until the late '60s and early '70s that art has been adopted by the fashion, design and music industries. Drawing on the heyday of the adoption of the arts by the media, Abetz & Drescher's world is a collage of its most famous examples. The background of *Electric Ladyland*, 2000, is filled with famous album covers by, among others, David Bowie, archetype of art school rock, as much known for his visual style as his music. The cover of *The Velvet Underground & Nico* which Andy Warhol designed in 1967 and which features just a banana and the artist's 'star' signature, appears also in the painting *Radiowellen*, 2000. Op art and its subsequent appropriation by fashion and design also pervades Abetz & Drescher's world in many forms, from TV to T-shirt designs.

All of these elements conjure up the lifestyle of a star as we know it through the media. The desire to live as our heroes live, to be our idols, comes to all of us in moments of reverie, when watching TV or listening to music. In their work Abetz & Drescher translate these desires into a critical mass of images, in doing so suggesting the very formation of 'cross-over' where everything is sampled and reconstituted on a daily basis. Chris Hammonds

## Dave Allen, Douglas Gordon & Jonathan Monk

Born Glasgow, 1963. Lives and works in Berlin.
Born Glasgow, 1966. Lives and works in New York.
Born Leicester, 1969. Lives and works in Berlin.

*Dance Practice,* 1996
Still from DVD
Courtesy the artists and
Lisson Gallery, London

Dave Allen, Douglas Gordon and Jonathan Monk are three artists whose work shares a common relationship to popular culture through music, cinema and television. Their individual practices often use simple structures to deconstruct the media, invited to work collaboratively, both the videos in *Air Guitar* are the result of the three artists 'jamming' together in a makeshift rehearsal studio.

In *Stooges Burn-Out*, 1995, the camera focuses on a lit cigarette inserted between a string and the tuning peg on the neck of a guitar. Placed in this way the cigarette waits as we do for the searing guitar solo that we come to expect when the lead guitarist puts smoking to one side for the music. However, this moment of anticipation is never rewarded. We continue to wait and the cigarette remains untouched. As it burns slowly down to its filter over the course of the nine-minute video, the band play The Stooges' *I Wanna Be Your Dog* over and over again, deferring the climax.

*Dance Practice*, 1995, takes as its subject another rock stereotype, the singer going wild on stage. In a rehearsal room, as the almost unseen band plays the intro to Nirvana's *Smells Like Teen Spirit*, a figure leaps into the frame but never sings. Instead the band repeats the intro and the figure goes wild again as if practicing a dance routine. As fatigue sets in from his exertion, the frontman seems obsessed with his image in a continual search for the right balance of energy and spectacle.

Both *Stooges Burn-Out* and *Dance Practice* take as their cue the moments at a gig when the crowd goes wild and all hell breaks loose in the 'mosh pit'. Those hedonistic surges of energy which seem to electrify everyone in the room — the searing guitar solo or the intro to the hit song — suspends every-thing else. By continually repeating or deferring these moments Allen, Douglas and Monk attempt to sustain those very instances of adrenaline and excitement. But these moments are by their very nature fleeting and their repetition turns them into humdrum. Chris Hammonds

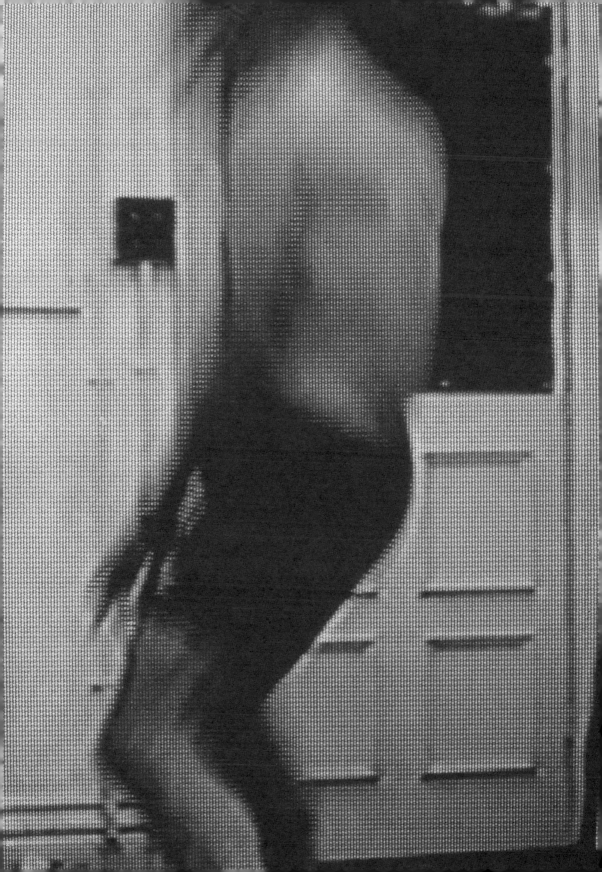

# Dave Allen and Ross Sinclair

Born Glasgow, 1963. Lives and works in Berlin.
Born Glasgow, 1966. Lives and works in Glasgow.

*The Sound of Young Scotland No.1
Part 1*, 1997
VHS tape and drawings
(installation shot)
Courtesy The Agency, London

*Jesus*, 1997
Still from VHS tape
Courtesy The Agency, London

'Bedroom learning' is a phrase coined by Ross Sinclair to articulate the teenage desire for freedom of expression. Much of the work Sinclair made collaboratively with Dave Allen in the mid '90s sees them revisiting this concept, recalling the songs they used to play in an introspective bid to find something to hang on to. However, rather than prescribing individuality, the very nature of 'bedroom learning' denotes the individual's role in the consumption of a mass-mediated culture industry. By embracing this concept their work lays bare the mechanics of the music industry. They play with the modus operandi of an aspiring garage rock band to disclose the conventions behind the myth.

Shot with a hand-held roving camera and set in a makeshift rehearsal space in Dave Allen's studio, *The Sound of Young Scotland No. 1 Part 1*, 1997, features the two protagonists jamming together on guitar and drums. The narrative follows the pair as they pick up a song riff, jam together, stop, start again, take a swig of beer and so forth for the duration of a three hour video tape. Every so often they stop what they are doing to scrawl song lyrics and sentences onto the walls behind them. Gradually, a narrative begins to take shape from the various soundbites delineating a rock trajectory from the Sex Pistols to AC/DC to Nirvana. The penultimate line of the accompanying text painted on the wall behind the monitor reads: 'They are 27 years old with nothing left to say.' Uncannily, this statement also portends the suicide of Kurt Cobain who in 1994 (the year the work was made), at the tender age of 27, blew his head off with a shotgun believing that he too had nothing left to say.

*Jesus*, 1997, a more mature and considered sequel to *The Sound of Young Scotland No. 1 Part 1*, depicts the artists jamming together again several years later. Only this time a static camera films them as they sit bare-foot on a bed, drinking tea resting on a amplifier and methodically trying to figure out the musical arrangement for The Velvet Underground track *Jesus*. The three year gap between the making of the two works marks a transition from wannabe rock stars, jumping about, flaunting their allegiances, to more resigned and somber individuals searching within themselves for meaning and reassurance. The off-the-cuff style of both works celebrates their unwavering relationship with the music, with each other and with the camera. Emma Mahony

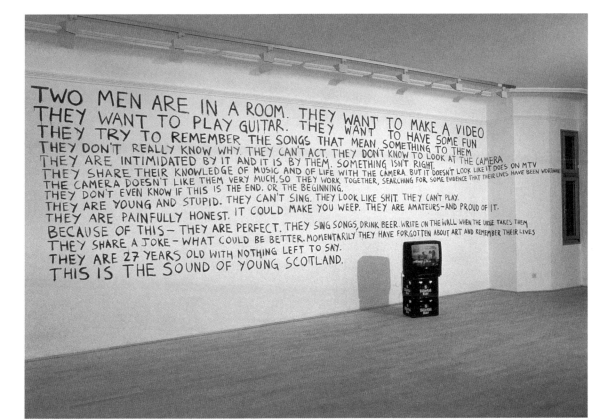

TWO MEN ARE IN A ROOM. THEY WANT TO MAKE A VIDEO
THEY WANT TO PLAY GUITAR. THEY WANT TO HAVE SOME FUN
THEY TRY TO REMEMBER THE SONGS THAT MEAN SOMETHING TO THEM
THEY DON'T REALLY KNOW WHY. THEY CAN'T ACT. THEY DON'T KNOW TO LOOK AT THE CAMERA
THEY ARE INTIMIDATED BY IT AND IT IS BY THEM. SOMETHING ISN'T RIGHT.
THEY SHARE THEIR KNOWLEDGE OF MUSIC AND OF LIFE WITH THE CAMERA. BUT IT DOESN'T LOOK LIKE IT DOES ON MTV
THE CAMERA DOESN'T LIKE THEM VERY MUCH. SO THEY WORK TOGETHER, SEARCHING FOR SOME EVIDENCE THAT THEIR LIVES HAVE BEEN WORTHWHILE
THEY DON'T EVEN KNOW IF THIS IS THE END. OR THE BEGINNING.
THEY ARE YOUNG AND STUPID. THEY CAN'T SING. THEY LOOK LIKE SHIT. THEY CAN'T PLAY.
THEY ARE PAINFULLY HONEST. IT COULD MAKE YOU WEEP. THEY ARE AMATEURS—AND PROUD OF IT.
BECAUSE OF THIS— THEY ARE PERFECT. THEY SING SONGS, DRINK BEER. WRITE ON THE WALL WHEN THE URGE TAKES THEM
THEY SHARE A JOKE— WHAT COULD BE BETTER. MOMENTARILY THEY HAVE FORGOTTEN ABOUT ART AND REMEMBER THEIR LIVES
THEY ARE 27 YEARS OLD WITH NOTHING LEFT TO SAY.
THIS IS THE SOUND OF YOUNG SCOTLAND.

# Luke Caulfield

**Born London, 1969. Lives and works in London.**

*Wanowan*, 2001
Oil on linen
172 x 172 cm
Courtesy the artist

*Ride to Live/Live to Ride*, 2000
Oil on linen
344 x 172 cm
Private Collection, London

Luke Caulfield's painting and photography are concerned with the coexistence of past, present and future through memory. Drawing analogies with heavy metal mythology, his paintings simultaneously present real and fictional worlds.

One such myth claims that if you play records backwards you can hear Satan's voice. In his recent series of photographs, Caulfield has drawn a visual analogy to this rite. In a playground, youths wearing heavy metal T-shirts travel up slides and spin anti-clockwise on the roundabout. As the figures blur with motion, only one T-shirt's image remains, a laughing skull floating menacingly in midair.

These heavy metal T-shirts are recurring motifs throughout Caulfield's works, bringing together the arcane and the mundane, biblical scenes of hellfire with the boredom of suburban teenagers. It is in this confusion of mythical and real time that Caulfield suggests the process of nostalgia and the many ways in which we transport ourselves from the present to the past. For Caulfield this is an arcane process of divination, one that never allows full recollection, memories remain fragmentary and intangible. The adolescents in his photographs are on the border between childhood and adult-hood, they mark the separation of our past and future lives.

In Caulfield's paintings this separation between what we are becoming and what we have been is present in a line of symmetry bisecting the canvas. As the figures look down on us like young gods, they do so in an evenly balanced manner: cigarettes hang from both sides of the mouth and both hands make secret signs. Likewise the T-shirts contain a hidden doubling. *Ride to Live, Live to Ride*, 1999, named after the legendary T-shirts, reflects in words the subtle corruption of original ideas, or sins, with those later learned. Equally in *Wanowan*, 2002, we are left to wonder if it is the young man that copies the image of the T-shirt or vice versa. The meticulously painted surface offers no clue, the resulting sensation is of a picture in a picture, a gateway to another dimension in a simple fabric print.

Confronted by these young men attempting to assert their maturity and independence, we are also faced with nostalgia for what we have left behind, memories now coloured by experience. An effect Caulfield likens to a photograph torn in two, the image and the tear both hinting at a story.

Chris Hammonds

# Sean Dower

Born Walsall, 1965. Lives and works in London.

Sean Dower in collaboration
with Martin Shiel & Richard Wilson
*Ronnie and Jimmy*, 2001
Stills from DVD
Courtesy the artist
with thanks to Lyle Perkins

Artist and musician Sean Dower has played in the now defunct Dick Donkey's Dawn, a guitar and electronic-based collaboration with fellow artists Georgina Starr and Oliver Hangl. Since the late '80s Dower has also been playing drums with artist Richard Wilson, collaboration beginning as part of the Bow Gamelan Ensemble, which played avant-garde contemporary music sometimes based on old barges traveling up and down the Thames. Dower and Wilson struck up a friendship based on their mutual passion for the drums; this continues today through weekly rehearsals, where they play drums together on two kits without accompaniment. These sessions are investigative and have influenced the duo's art practices and occasionally emerging in experimental live performances and collaborative video pieces.

In Dower's video work *Ronnie and Jimmy*, 2001, his weekly rehearsals with Wilson provide an extreme musical backdrop to an oblique story. The original concept was developed with the filmmaker Martin Shiel and features two men wearing Jimmy Carter and Ronald Reagan masks holding a conversation in a car while inhaling helium and careering at full revs round a derelict car park. From time to time, the film cuts to footage of Dower and Wilson playing drums wearing the same masks. What seems at first to be the work of two bored guys goofing around, begins to make sense through references to films such as Gillo Pontecorvo's 1965 opus *The Battle of Algiers* and the conversation between the two 'presidents', barely audible beneath the heavy soundtrack.

The integration of music and video is an essential part of Dower's art practice. The sound and image are intertwined in video works such as *Music in Trees*, 2001. For this short work the artist collected lengths of cassette tapes found discarded around East London. In his studio the tapes were cut up and spliced together at random resulting in a surprisingly consistent piece of music from the found fragments. This then formed the soundtrack for a video of Dower climbing a tree in which one of the tapes was suspended. The work attempts to reconcile video and music cassettes through the editing process, sound and image influencing one another.

Chris Hammonds

# Sam Durant

**Born Seattle, 1961. Lives and works in Los Angeles.**

*Partially Buried 1960s/70s: Utopia Reflected; Partially Buried 1960s/70s: Distopia Revealed*, 1998
Mirrors, dirt, cassette players, cassette loops
Each 51 x 213 x 101 cm
Courtesy the artist and Blum & Poe, Santa Monica

*Neil Young #2*, 1999
Graphite on paper
76 x 56 cm
Courtesy Wilhelm Schuermann

Sam Durant, like Robert Smithson before him, is engaged in an investigation of the law of entropy. But where Smithson's work largely considered the effects of entropy upon nature — how it is the nature of matter to break down and come to a state of rest — Durant examines how these forces are steadily wearing away at culture. Taking '60s America as his starting point, his work examines how its ideals collapsed.

Smithson's *Partially Buried Woodshed*, 1970, is a useful starting point in a discussion of Durant's work. Several months after Smithson made the work at Kent State University, four students were killed by the National Guard firing on unarmed Vietnam War protesters. Smithson's *Non-Site* became a figurative gravesite, an underground monument to the killings and a foreshadowing of Smithson's own death in a plane crash three years later.

Sam Durant's *Partially Buried 1960s/70s: Utopia Reflected; Partially Buried 1960s/70s: Distopia Revealed*, 1998, reflects upon one of the more enduring myths of the '60s, the utopia that was Woodstock and the distopia that befell Altamont. The installation comprises earth piled onto two mirrors which are lying on the floor (recalling Smithson's 1969 rock-salt and mirror *Non-Sites*), the voices of Wavy Gravy and Mick Jagger can be heard emanating from two tape players hidden under the dirt. Wavy Gravy, a member of the counterculture collective who distributed food for free

in the '60s, can be heard addressing the joyous revelers at Woodstock: 'You've been really groovy, and you are making the scene.' In stark contrast, Jagger addresses the strung out and rioting crowd at Altamont with a nervous plea:

> Why are we fighting?! Why are we fighting?! We don't want to fight! *Come on!* Who wants to fight? Every other scene has been cool... Let's just get it together! ... everyone, Hell's Angels, everybody, let's just keep ourselves together.

But Jagger's plea falls on deaf ears as the gun wielding concertgoer Meredith Hunter is stabbed and kicked to death by a Hell's Angel security guard as The Stones play *Under My Thumb*.

By presenting us with a string of scenarios, Durant seeks to represent allegorically the entropic events set in motion by the killings at Altamont and Kent State which escalated into the political and social upheaval of the period. His drawings and sculptures after Smithson and their scatological captions, often mirrored and reversed, trace links from post-minimalism to popular culture, from Kent State to Altamont, The Rolling Stones, Neil Young, Kurt Cobain and back again to Robert Smithson. Neil Young enters the picture with *My My, Hey Hey, (Out of the Blue)/(Into the Black)*, written partly as a result of Altamont and partly as a tribute to the dead Sex Pistol Sid Vicious. Durant draws a further link to Kurt Cobain, who appropriated Young's lyrics 'It's better to burn out then fade away' in his suicide note.

Emma Mahony

Kurt Cobain

# Peter Harris

**Born Portsmouth, 1967. Lives and works in London.**

*Hard Rain Gig*, 2001
Watercolour drawings on paper
Each 35.5 x 25.4 cm
Courtesy the artist and
Andrew Mummery, London

Over the past two years Peter Harris has been documenting his life in watercolour, recording significant and insignificant moments ranging from the mundane to the melodramatic, each event painstakingly recreated with a hobbyist's attention to detail.

Harris's work often involves experimenting with new ways of making self-portraits, many of which become collaborations. For his *Self-Portrait by Proxy* series Harris invited members of his family and cultural icons who have had an influence on his life to give him ideas for paintings, searching for his identity through those who had played a part in constructing it. While gathering responses from sources ranging from his sister to Tony Hart and David Bowie, there were a few significant absentees, most notably The Clash and Sid Vicious, who, either unable or unwilling to enter into this collaboration, were sadly represented in the exhibition

by name plaques inscribed with the date that they entered Harris's psyche.

In the work *Hard Rain (traditional)*, 2001, Harris paid further tribute to the role that music has played in his life, combining his own anecdotal song lyrics with multiple references to protest songs, personalising them in order to vent his pent up frustrations with the bourgeois commercialism of the post–YBA art world. Bob Dylan's original *A Hard Rain's a-Gonna Fall*, 1963, was written in protest of the Cuban Missile Crisis, at a time when Dylan and many others felt that they were about to witness the end of the world, concentrating as much mate-rial as possible into one song. Harris's version is similarly condensed, although lacking Dylan's time pressure — he wrote his over six months — it con-jures up experiences from this period in a rambling semi-diaristic manner. Borrowing the chorus of *A Hard Rain's a-Gonna Fall* and further lyrics from

The Clash, Harris sets his own song to the music of The Clash's 1977 anthem *White Riot*. In true DIY style, Harris painted a mock Clash backdrop of flags and his hybrid song was performed by The Clash tribute band (Black Market Clash), before a hot, sweaty, pogoing crowd of screaming fans, held in the secret venue of a friend's spacious front room. Harris's low budget film of the proceedings attempts to replicate the authenticity of the punk endeavour. The cameraman jumps up and down with the fans coming in an out of focus in a private homage to *The Punk Rock Movie*, Don Letts's 1977 directorial foray into the punk scene.  Emily Pethick

# Paul Housley

Born Stalybridge, 1964. Lives and works in London.

*Trans*, 2002
Oil on canvas
40.5 x 51 cm
Courtesy the artist
and Nylon, London

*Home-made*, 2002
Badges
Dimensions variable
Courtesy the artist
and Nylon, London

Paul Housley paints everyday events and extra-ordinary moments: cat's eyes in close-up, a man on the moon, The Beatles' *White Album* on cassette, the endless highway depicted on the sleeve of the Kraftwerk album *Autobahn*. These images are painterly in a very conventional sense, with neither the pretence of photographic realism nor the mimicry of spatial reality. Housley asserts a painterliness in a world of simulated experience and these pieces enjoy the declaration of their medium.

Housley's subjects deal with substitution: role-playing, dressing up and dressing down, momen-tarily pretending to be someone else. The lived language of rock is borne out in Housley's painted world. While the possibility of being another, feel-ing for another, is heard in the whispers, shouts and screams of rock music, the muted empathy is stored in the material culture it spawns. Housley collects memories and invents a common past for us, imbuing his paintings with personal relevance within the recognisable bric-a-brac of both domestic and popular culture. Indeed the success of popular culture as a shaping idiom of identity can be reduced to its wit in relating the material

world of memorabilia, relics and recordings of one kind or another to a personal account of time. Housley reflects upon this in his bright intimate paintings with similar resonance. The presence of the visual in rock culture is immediate: the ragged concert ticket, the poster, the album cover, the torn-out magazine interview are all semblances of the band and clues to the music.

The evident technique of Housley's paintings, with their textured clean colours and obvious brush strokes, is in keeping with the simplicity of the rock myth that trades on promoting apparent idiosyncratic expression. There is innocence in a fantasy world that emphasises adolescent imaginings, where desires are played out in music alluding to the spectrum of human emotion. Housley's paintings describe a moment in the past that we all experienced at one time or another. His images epitomise the raw integrity of the rock endeavour, the production of a moment where most dreams seem possible and their reflections ever collectable. Niamh Ann Kelly

New York
London
and
Stalybridge

Enjoy
Nihilism.

taurus

ENglanD
NEEDS ME BUT
I canT get ouT
OF BEd

# Scott King

Born East Yorkshire, 1969. Lives and works in London.

Joy Division, 2 May 1980, High Hall,
The University of Birmingham, England,
1999
Inkjet print
102 x 152 cm
Courtesy Magnani, London

Scott King works as both an artist and graphic designer. Currently the creative director of the magazine Sleazenation, his résumé also boasts the art direction of i-D magazine, the design of Malcolm McLaren's London mayoral campaign, the artwork for Pet Shop Boys' single *Home and Dry* and work for the band Earl Brutus. King regularly collaborates with journalist Matt Worley as *Crash!*, which has taken such forms as a regular four-page spread in Sleazenation, a sporadic publication of the same name and an exhibition at the ICA in London subtitled *Corporatism and Complicity*. *Crash!* sets out to condemn the very culture it is subsumed within, mocking '90s corporate lifestyle culture, the commodification of youth culture and the coercion of protest culture, with slogans like 'Prada Meinhof' loudly proclaiming 'death to the new'.

King's critique also extends to music and the corporate structures behind rock bands. *Into the Black*, 2000, presents the tragic deaths of rock stars Ian Curtis, Richey Edwards and Kurt Cobain within the clinical format of marketing charts. In reducing the passionate, lonely desperation of these stars to mere facts and figures, King derides the calculated way that record companies profit from the mythologised deaths of their stars, most of which unglamorously took place in their own homes.

In the series *Dot Gigs*, King pays tribute to concerts that became turning points in rock history, most of which relate to deaths. Namely, the last Joy Division gig before Ian Curtis killed himself; The Stones' concert at Altamont, which symbolically marked the end of the hippie era; the Hammersmith Odeon gig of 1973 where David Bowie 'killed off' Ziggy Stardust; the last Manic Street Preachers concert before Richey Edwards disappeared; the last Sex Pistols gig in San Francisco before Sid Vicious died and The Who's concert in Woodstock, which helped them break into the US market. Using the most basic representational system to record the spectacle of these gigs, King reduces both the bands and their audiences to graphic dots. By making the dots which symbolise the audience the same size as their stage idols, he also attempts to bring the overblown status of these bands back down to the level of their fans.

If King had been a few years younger he might have been present at these concerts. His work betrays a slight sense of melancholy in being one generation too late. With the Joy Division lyric 'love will tear us apart' tattooed on his forearm, King cannot help but be a product of and a slave to a myth. Emily Pethick

Joy Division, 2 May 1980, High Hall, The University of Birmingham, England

# Christian Marclay

Born California, 1955. Lives and works in New York.

*Hot August Night*
(from the series *Body Mix*), 1991
Altered album covers, thread
58 x 33 cm
Courtesy Paula Cooper Gallery,
New York

*Mad*
(from the series *Body Mix*), 1991
Altered album covers, thread
89 x 51 cm
Courtesy Paula Cooper Gallery,
New York

Whilst studying sculpture at Massachusetts College of Art in the late '70s Christian Marclay made frequent trips to New York where he became familiar with the work of Dan Graham and Laurie Anderson through the punk rock club circuit, trips which would subsequently inform his all-encompassing oeuvre as artist, musician, curator and turntablist. Marclay has released several solo and compilation albums including *Records 1981–89*, a collection of some of his more obscure recordings and performances, and has collaborated with musicians such as John Zorn, Shelley Hirsch and Sonic Youth.

Marclay first began working with vinyl records in the late '70s cutting them into strips and re-assembling them, scratching them and sticking tape or stickers onto their surfaces. By modifying what was once a mass-produced commodity, he attempts to reinscribe the vinyl disc with a unique value. This, in turn, bled into his live performances where, working with between four and eight turntables some of which rigged to play backwards,

he would use the newly authored records to achieve original acoustic scores.

In a logical progression he turned his attention to the records packaging and began collaging and reworking record sleeves. This inspired his *Skin Mix* series where body parts of musicians from various sleeves are combined in Frankenstein-like hybrids. *Bad Boy*, 1992, merges the naked torso of Iggy Pop from the sleeve of *New Values* with the legs of the unidentified female on the cover of Bad Boys' *Private Party*. *Hot August Night*, 1991, unites the torso of Neil Diamond strumming an air guitar with a pair of female legs in an almost flawless seam. The series seeks to reveal the ideological assumptions encoded in the seemingly neutral field of a record sleeve by highlighting the role pornography, androgyny and 'camp' decadence, as much as the music itself, played in defining the overall 'package' that was the '70s glam rock industry.

Emma Mahony

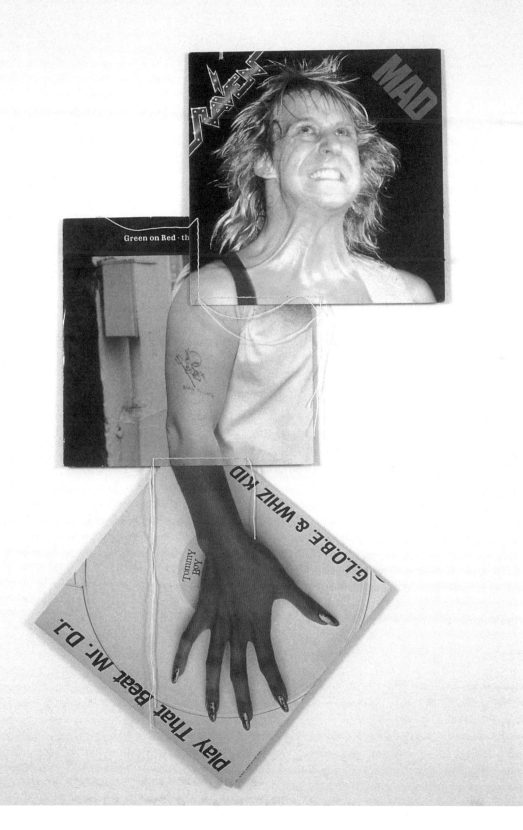

# Paul McDevitt

**Born Troon, Scotland, 1972. Lives and works in London.**

*Untitled (mirror lake)*, 2000
Acrylic on Post-It
12.5 x 7.7 cm
Private Collection, Turin

*Wrist Action (Religious Drawing)*, 2000
Biro on MDF
120 x 150 cm
Collection of the British Museum,
London

The method of production Paul McDevitt applies to his paintings and drawings has its equivalent in work of bands that make heavy use of music samples such as Public Enemy, Beastie Boys and the musician/producer/turntablist DJ Shadow. McDevitt in fact takes a similar approach to creating something new out of pre-existing elements.

DJ Shadow, a groundbreaker in sample-based musical composition, has been an influence of particular importance on McDevitt's practice. In his debut album, *Endtroducing*, 1996, DJ Shadow re-orchestrated music that already existed, being the first person to release an album consisting entirely of old material but yet succeeding to create a fresh sound.

The creative process behind McDevitt's drawings is not dissimilar. He initially works digitally, building an image on computer out of heterogeneous fragments, using a mix of found images, existing drawings, photographs etc., which he scans in or finds on the web. The resulting image — created through a process of collaging or 'sampling' — is not the artwork but a visual reference for the final drawings. Using ballpoint pens, biros or coloured pencils, he creates intricately rendered, layered drawings, similarly to what DJ Shadow terms 'reconstruction from the ground up'.

Another strand of McDevitt's work is an on-going series of paintings on Post-It notes. The minuscule acrylic works deal with a whole range of subjects from lunar landscapes to the exterior of the notorious 'crack house' in McDevitt's neighbourhood. He has even painted interior views imagining what the occupants of the crack house might be doing to while away the hours. Almost invisible, the fragile Post-It notes hang unobtrusively on the wall and surprise the viewer with their alternative Lilliputian world. They, like McDevitt's other drawings, succeed in making something truly epic out of humble materials.

More recently the artist has started working on a series of paintings which utilise rock T-shirts as their subject matter. Second-hand T-shirts emblazoned with the slogans of bands such as Bon Jovi or Bruce Springsteen are stretched like canvas, then sprayed and modified. The resulting images are real, punky and home made, everything that such bands are not. Just as DJ Shadow gives new life to old sounds, McDevitt makes his own attempt to infuse images of Bon Jovi and Bruce Springsteen with some creativity. Elisabetta Fabrizi

# Dave Muller

**Born San Francisco, 1964. Lives and works in Los Angeles.**

*An Ending*, 2001
Coloured pencil on paper
81 x 102 cm
Collection of Kenneth Freed

The work of Dave Muller is a resourceful negotiation and celebration of artistic communities and the events and documents through which they are promoted, enacted and historicised. In the years before he transformed his studio at Cal Arts into a venue for impromptu exhibitions by fellow students, his career as a college radio DJ ignited his interest in playfully connecting the work of others to his own open-ended artistic systems.

In 1994 he orchestrated the first *Three Day Weekend*, an ongoing series of nomadic, grass roots events in which Muller invites other artists he admires to exhibit works in the company of music, beer and an effusive audience. Each exhibition is structured around a loose theme or set of possibilities which frequently magnifies Muller's interest in contesting notions of authorship and proposing more vital, unencumbered topographies of collaboration and exchange. Taking place most often in the artist's Los Angeles studio or home, but increasingly in locations as far afield as New York, Tokyo and Berlin, the events chart the immaterial architecture of their own transitory social and cultural moment. They are social sculptures with a soundtrack, usually provided by Muller's own hand at the turntables or by art bands like The Red Krayola and Destroy All Monsters.

At stake in the *Three Day Weekend* programme

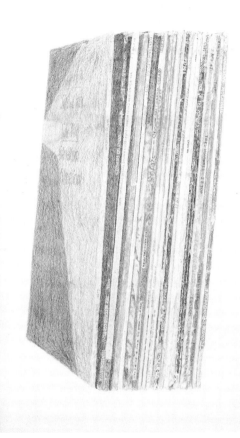

is the nature of promotion and a question about how artworks are staged in time, social space and the chain of cultural authority. Muller also spins these notions into his own DIY information technology: a series of watercolours and drawings he produces based on gallery invitations, event flyers and other printed promotional ephemera. If *Three Day Weekend* provides a time-based model of fleeting cultural relationships, then the paintings flag up the ironies of trying to document such intangible events. Like the flyers which marked LA's vital punk scene on phone poles and bus shelters all over town, marketing material in the art world frequently outlives the events it serves to adver-

tise in the first place. It also allows enthusiasts like Muller a chance to archive the transitory culture in which he operates. By painting and subtly altering these documents and then exhibiting them as 'art', Muller publicly reactivates his archive much as he does when he pulls a record from the stacks to play it at a *Three Day Weekend*. Using his role as catalyst and the reproduction of images and sounds, he reformulates the art world's mechanics of promotion and display into a more open system. It is one based on generosity, wry humour and conviction. Stuart Comer

# Seamus Nicolson

Born London, 1971, lives and works in London.

Sam, 1996
C-Print mounted on aluminium
101 x 152 cm
Courtesy The Agency, London

Mike, 2000
C-Print mounted on aluminium
101 x 154 cm
Courtesy The Agency, London

Seamus Nicolson's work focuses on anonymous moments of everyday life, in particular urban, nocturnal life in London. Shot mostly in medium format, or occasionally with a snapshot camera, the large-scale photographs have as their protagonists young anonymous characters that are in a moment of transition, both emotionally and spatially; they are lost in some kind of reverie or daydream, the city is as surreal as they feel, its appearance at night reflecting their inner experiences.

Music is an oblique reference in Nicolson's work. It is present as a reference to youth culture, capturing that moment in someone's life when music plays a very important role. The age when identity is shaped, when the type of music one listens to is something that one might use to distinguish oneself. When he was still a student at the Royal College of Art, Nicolson took a picture from a balcony in a club, capturing on film a moment when urban youth is unified by music. Surprised by the result he continued photographing clubbers until his work finally progressed out of the clubs into the city, tracing the journeys people find themselves on.

In Nicolson's photographs music is present by means of its absence. What we see is the moment when the music is no longer there but is still echoing in the character's head. Sam, 1996, was just a snap taken after a party. A friend of the artist, Sam was spontaneously performing for Nicolson. Always carrying a camera, the artist, engaged by Sam's drunken movements, made the perfect snap of a particular moment in the life of his friend.

Nicolson's photos oscillate between the constructed and the spontaneous. Mike, 2000, originally taken as a band publicity shot, is far more contrived than Sam. It is a mixture of the staged and the uncalculated, where the environment dictates the lighting. Mike's face is lit by the car light and the light illuminating the girl's T-shirt is thrown upwards from the Gameboy she is holding, resulting in a long staged exposure mixed with ambient light.

Location and character are of equal importance in Nicolson's work. The process starts with Nicolson seeing a place which interests him, finding 'the stage', then setting about looking for the right person to fit that stage and to act his own imaginary suspended narratives, a process which can take a long time as Nicolson never uses models or actors. The situations Nicolson recreates are a combination of elements he has encountered and elements he has imagined, a mixture of fiction and documentary. Elisabetta Fabrizi

## James Pyman
Born Eastbourne, 1962. Lives and works in London.

The Slits, 1999
Pencil on paper
106 x 112 cm
Courtesy Cabinet Gallery, London

James Pyman makes labour intensive, black and white, large-scale drawings. What unites the works, which are sometimes lyrical, sometimes surreal, sometimes cartoonish is a sense of nostalgia, a feeling of melancholy.

Music is one of the subjects of Pyman's work, an important yet not exclusive influence. His drawings often make reference to the music he was listening to while growing up, from Joy Division to The Birthday Party to The Pop Group, underground bands at the time, far from the mainstream. Despite the fact that these bands are remembered and loved primarily for their lyrics teeming with tragic feelings of loss and desperation, their image was, most importantly, overpoweringly visual and it is precisely this visual power which influences Pyman's art.

*The Birthday Party*, 1995, the first and only painting Pyman ever produced, is a painting of a concert by The Birthday Party which Pyman went to in 1981, the striking stage presence of a young Nick Cave lingering in the artist's head and soul ever since. *1979*, 1996, is a drawing originally commissioned for an exhibition called *Kiss This* which took place on St Valentine's Day 1996. Being asked to make a work about love, Pyman produced a drawing of a school desk on which a heart is engraved, containing the first names of the members of Joy

Division. Not an ironic work, the drawing plays with the overloaded melancholic feelings associated with the school desk. Its title refers to a very specific moment in time. Joy Division had a brief career, having made their first record in 1977 and their last in 1980, as shortly after Ian Curtis, their charismatic lead singer, committed suicide.

In *1979* music is compared to first love. The drawing is not only full of melancholy in its rendering of a teenager's discovery of passion, but it is also extremely tragic, just as Joy Division's own history is. *The Slits*, 1999, on the other hand, recalls the student pastime of copying a favourite band record cover to occupy the mind during a tedious lesson. The drawing is a copy of a photograph of The Slits (an all-girl punk band active between 1976 and 1979) taken by influential rock photographer Penny Smith, part of a very controversial session she did with the band for NME in 1979. The original image was reproduced on a very small scale and in colour, by reproducing it as a drawing and making it life-size, Pyman elevates a tiny moment to museum scale. Heightened by the use of the black and white, the work becomes historical and, scaled with the viewers, faces them on the same level to convey real memories. Elisabetta Fabrizi

## George Shaw

Born Coventry, 1966. Lives and works in Nottingham.

*Bags*, 1999
Acrylic on rucksacks
Dimensions variable
Collection of the artist

*The English Malady*, 2002
Pencil drawing on paper
42 x 59.4 cm
Courtesy Anthony Wilkinson Gallery,
London

Processed as they are by the artist's personal vision, George Shaw's paintings of Coventry's housing estates could allude to the suburbs of any English town. The soulless architecture, rain sodden streets, muddy copses and leaden skies of his recollections share the gray uniformity typical of post war suburbia. Rendered in great detail in Humbrol enamel paint, their vacant glossy sheen lends them a sinister edge. This, coupled with the absence of human presence, conjures the darker side of suburbia. The only sign that their might have been life in this ghost town is suggested by the dimly lit graffiti on the walls of *The Subway*, 1998, and the orange glow radiating from inside the building in *The Black Prince*, 1999, but for the most part Shaw denies our access with tightly pulled net curtains and blackened windows.

There is one particular cast of characters whose presence is suggested through their absence from Shaw's paintings. People like Chad (The Mod in *Quadrophenia*) and Mark E. Smith of The Fall who populated Shaw's imagination as he trudged the gray streets from the red brick school stopping off at the Knockout Fish Bar before making his way home. These are the characters with whom he would have aspired to walk the streets of Tile Hill

when he was growing up, the very people who would become the subject of his pencil drawings.

Too young for the tail end of punk, Shaw jumped childishly on the Mod Revival as it came through town. The Mods implied the kind of glamour Shaw desired. Chad, the Mod of Pete Townsend's imagination, is the subject of one of Shaw's latest drawings, *The English Malady*, 2002. In the booklet accompanying The Who's album *Quadrophenia* Chad was cast as a loner, an outsider; somebody who was searching for something that is located in the past, a longing that Shaw seems to empathise with. Never quite content to be simply a fan or an observer, Shaw draws himself into another world where characters like Chad and The Smiths take centre stage.

During his school days Shaw capitalised on his drawing skills by customising his classmates satchels with the logos of their favourite bands in return for money or school dinner tickets. Twenty years on and still drawing on his past allegiances, Shaw revisits his adolescent obsessions in *Bags*, 1999. 'Some of the bags are copies of the ones I remember making and others are what I would have made if I'd had the time, or could have been bothered, or hadn't grown up.' Emma Mahony

54

# Bob & Roberta Smith

Born London, 1964. Lives and works in London.

*I Believe in The Clash*, 1999
Vinyl silk and gloss on panel
61.5 x 82 cm
Private Collection, London

*I Believe in The Fall*, 1999
Vinyl silk and gloss on panel
45.5 x 61.5 cm
Courtesy Anthony Wilkinson Gallery,
London

Bob & Roberta Smith have taken their do it yourself moniker from the '70s punk movement. This is particularly true of their band The Ken Ardley Playboys which has been variously described as 'ramshackle sub punk' and 'a cross between The Fall and a gravel truck falling of Canary Wharf Tower'. Formed in 1992, the band trades on amateurism and failure.

Failure is a proposition which runs throughout Bob & Roberta's practice. Forefronted by works such as *Flawed*, 1996, a video of Bob launching a flotilla of concrete ships on the Serpentine and *Humiliate Bob Smith*, 1993, a video piece in which the artist recounts every humiliating episode in his artistic career from rejection by dealers to being told to 'piss off' by John Lennon outside the Dakota club.

*I Believe in the Clash*, *I Believe in the Fall* and *I Believe in Mel C.*, all 1999, are just some of the slogans that make up Bob & Roberta's trademark text paintings. Their declaration of unconditional belief in The Fall is understandable, particularly given that the music they compose for The Ken Ardley Playboys is derivative of The Falls' harsh sound. But to place ex Spice diva Mel C. on a similar footing begs a question or two. As it happens the work is a tribute not to the 'Sporty Spice' persona we are all so familiar with but to the post-split 'Alienated Spice'. The statement reflects her rather brief foray into the punk scene with the release of *Goin' Down*, one of those rare moments which Bob & Roberta believe is worthy of immortalising in their art.

Their latest series of borderline anarchic slogans borrow from the derogatory phrases you would hear bandied about in a children's playground to insult their contemporaries. 'Patti Smith is a pumpkin head', 'Dan Graham is a fish face' and 'Jasper Johns is a dinosaur' they variously declare.

Text paintings which tell misleading but amusing anecdotes about incongruous public figures have long been a part of their repertoire. *Mark E. Smith (Couldn't Get Ahead)*, 1995, is one of such fantastic fable, telling the unlikely story of Greenberg organising a lunch for Mike Kelley and his hero Mark E. Smith of The Fall, where the latter shouted abuse at Kelley: 'Don't Patronize me you fucking arty tosser.' Bob & Roberta leave us to ponder why artists try so hard to drag rock culture into art when rock is infinitely better than art could ever aspire to be. Emma Mahony

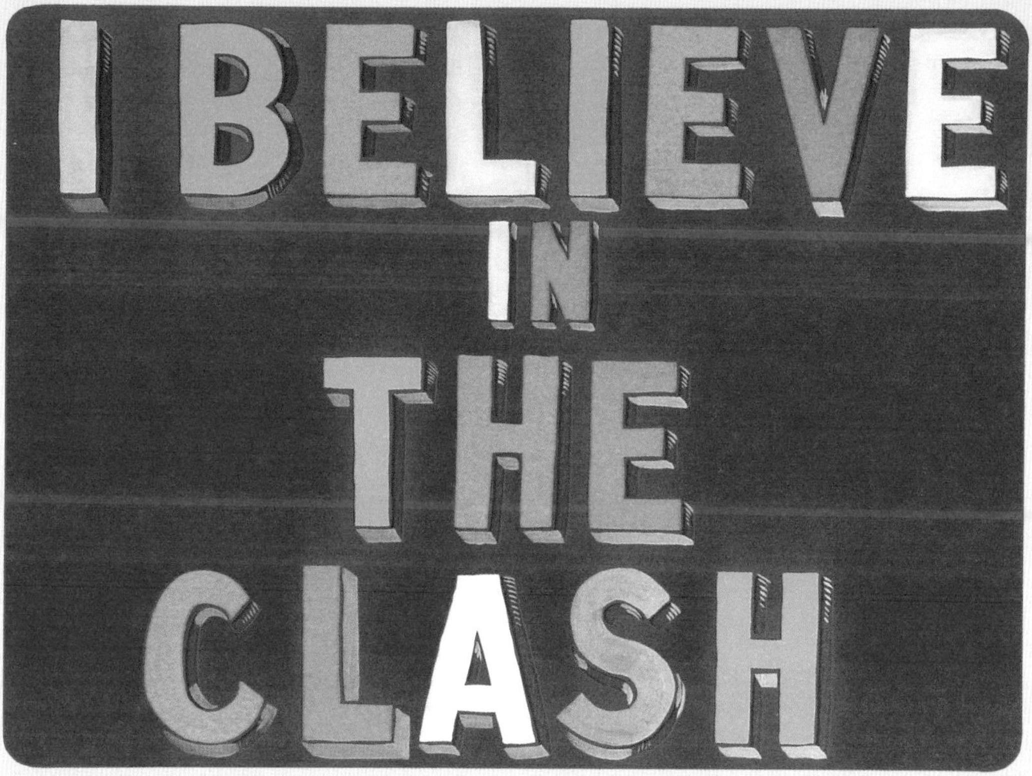
I BELIEVE
IN
THE
CLASH

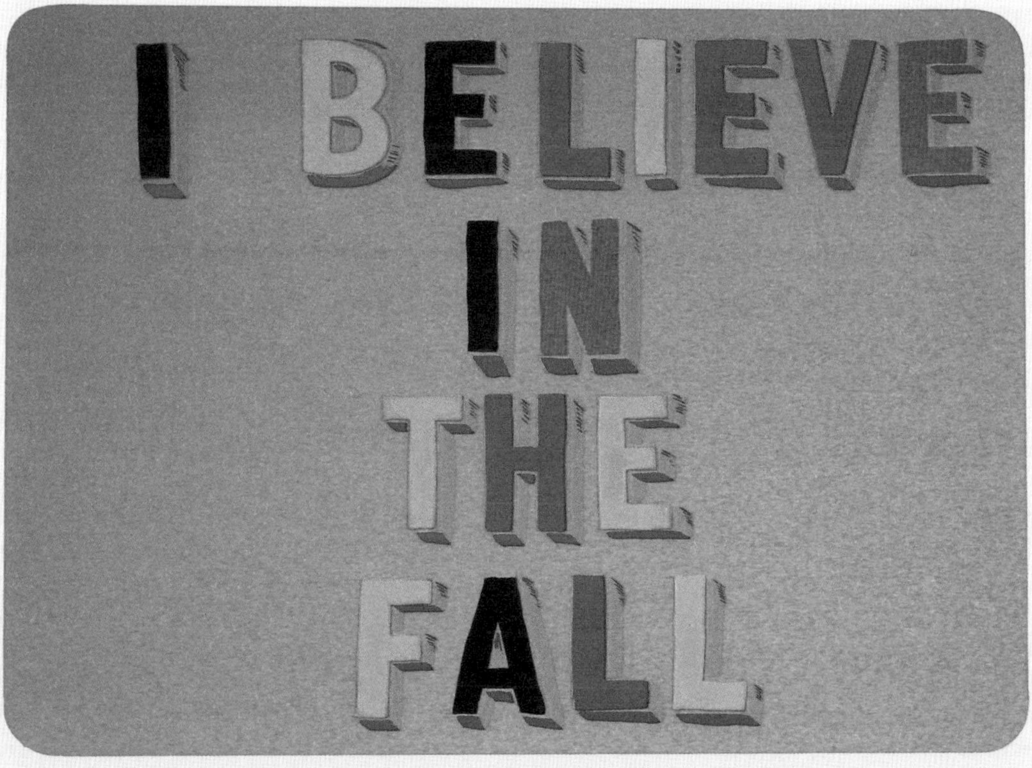
I BELIEVE
IN
THE
FALL

# Frances Stark

Born Newport Beach, California, 1967. Lives and works in Los Angeles.

*What Part of Now Don't You
Understand?*, 1999
Silkscreen on paper
45.5 x 58 cm
Courtesy greengrassi, London

Frances Stark's work hinges on what Raymond Pettibon calls 'the surprisingly big littleness of the excerpt.' The backbone of her practice consists of delicate, unassuming drawings and collages onto which she meticulously traces carbon copies of literary phrases and fragments of pop cultural information. Harvested from the writings of Robert Musil and Samuel Beckett, or a timeline of The Beatles' career, these texts are repeated across discrete sections on liberal expanses of paper. Recalling Robert Smithson's heaps of language and Carl Andre's concrete poetry, the patterns formed by Stark's mimetic activity quietly reverberate with a romance for the artist's voice.

Stark seems to invert Barthes's query 'how can anyone believe that a given work is an object independent of the psyche and personal history of the critic studying it?' Her work asserts its fascination with the construction of interiority, and her economical quotations delineate a precise universe of references that test the constitution of the self against the private and public reading of culture.

Her own relationship to that culture has manifested itself in a wide range of media. She has performed in lo-fi bands, presented works such as *One half hour of air*, 1998, on FM radio broadcasts, and appeared in films and videos by Raymond Pettibon and Charles Ray. Excerpts from her own wistful fan letters to rock stars like Pavement's Steven Malkmus have appeared in both her drawings and in an impressive body of experimental fiction. In 1999 she published *The Architect & The Housewife*, a meditation on design and domesticity and their complicity in the construction and maintenance of gender roles.

The most recent development in Stark's practice is a series of videos in which a stationary camera observes the artist's cats enacting their daily rituals amidst the slightly distressed and sun-dappled Danish furniture in her living room. Titles like *At the table with newspapers*, 2002, and *One minute on the couch*, 2001, reinforce the everyday nature of the videos and each piece is accompanied by a song that determines its duration. Ranging from music by The Velvet Underground to Björk and T.S.O.L., the songs intersect and frame the peripheral details of Stark's domestic life. *I'm just about to lose my mind*, 2002, features The Slits' cover of *I Heard it Through the Grapevine*. Whilst the cats begin to wage all-out civil war, The Slits' early feminist punk take on Motown inflects Stark's home with a desperate urgency. Just as the lexical punch of the text landscapes in the drawings almost overwhelms their reductive format, Stark's tidy apartment becomes an unwitting and momentary venue for girl-punk rage and feline apocalypse. Stuart Comer

# CHINATOWN, Los Angeles?

11.11.99

# John Strutton

**Born Bedford, 1966. Lives and works in London.**

*Guitars*, 2001–02
Gloss on guitars
Dimensions variable
Courtesy the artist and Nylon,
London

*Donkey Jacket Series*, 2001–02
Gloss on donkey jackets
Each 85 x 60 cm
Courtesy the artist and Nylon,
London

John Strutton is the front man of his own self-styled group The Band of Nod, an assembly of 40-plus all singing, all dancing guitar and kazoo players, which, like the ideology of punk, recruits members first and then lets them learn how to play later on. Described by the artist as an experiment in Dionysian behaviour, Strutton's intention with The Band of Nod was to find an armature to hang cult behaviour off. To such ends they perform a barely recognisable medley of cover versions kitted out variously as an army of Groucho Marx followers, a company of orange faced demented Oompa Loompa's from Roald Dahl's *Charlie and The Chocolate Factory* and a litter of spotted dogs from Disney's *101 Dalmatians*.

Strutton's work does more than simply mine the 'pop' cultural heritage of his youth, in itself an undertaking, but also draws from a very eclectic range of influences from Count Dracula and the Oompa Loompa's to The Daleks and Tony Hancock. For *I could have been somebody I just couldn't be bothered*, 2001, he enlisted actor Burt Kwouk, better known as Kato in *The Pink Panther* films, to do a live restaging of Tony Hancocks' *The Radio Ham*. The Band of Nod, with the artist's father on vocals, performed renditions of the Joy Division anthem *Love Will Tear Us Apart* and Softcell's *Bedsit Land*.

His series of painted guitars and Donkey jackets have a very immediate relationship to rock culture on both a conscious and subconscious level. The collective vernacular of rock'n'roll — the title of an album, a song lyric, artwork appropriated from a record sleeve, an anarchic slogan — comes together to tell a very personalized rock biography. A rough appropriation of the Go Feet record label is painted onto the back of one of his Donkey jackets, it also features on a guitar painted with slogans such as 'Dogma', 'Blind Faith', 'Do Nothing' and 'Fashion is my only Culture'. Other guitars, perhaps revealing a more fickle form of allegiance, are graffitied with mottoes and legends almost to saturation point then finished off with catch-phrases such as 'Take the Money and Run'.

In his recent series of drawings, the process of fabricating the work appears to be intrinsically related to the mechanics of music production. He has utilized a record player to manufacture a series of watercolour drawings of 7" singles. To make the work he places a sheet of watercolour paper on a turntable which he sets in motion, the resultant concentric circles mimic the grooves of a vinyl record with extraordinary accuracy, leaving the viewer to wonder what they would sound like if we could play them. Emma Mahony

# Jessica Voorsanger

Born New York, 1965. Lives and works in London.

*This one's about Whiskey*, 2000
Neon
28 x 163 x 21 cm
Courtesy Anthony Wilkinson Gallery,
London

Jessica Voorsanger's practice explores the mass
mediated culture industry. Her interests are
closely aligned with phenomenons of fandom and
she regularly assumes the guise of a devoted fan in
order to explore the mutually dependent relationship between the celebrity and his/her fan base.

The rare moments of communion at a concert
when the onstage stars condescend to address
their screaming fans is the subject of an ongoing
series of acrylic on paper signs and neon text
works by Voorsanger. On such occasions the revel-
ers in the mosh-pit below the stage lap up every
word, as though it was addressed directly to them,
like a hungry congregation at a Baptist sermon.
'Good Evening Planet Earth' – Oasis' address to
the nation when their concert was transmitted live
on Radio 1 in August 1996 – betrays an arrogance
typical of '90s pop celebrity. By extricating these
statements from the context in which they were

first spoken, Voorsanger allows them to be read as the megalomaniac bunkum that they really are. *This one's about Whiskey*, 2000, attributed to Shane MacGowan at a Pogues concert in Dublin in 1986, offers a less than insightful introduction to what one could probably guess refers to the track *Streams of Whiskey*. In her more recent works the text has been painstakingly embroidered on silk producing a bizarre juxtaposition between the 'reserved' craft of embroidery and the brash rock'n'roll statements they convey. Eric Faulkner announces his disquiet to a fan with the half-jokey/half-serious: 'Hey mate! You think you have it bad, I used to be a Bay City Roller!' In another, David Cassidy's 'Do you know who I am?' address to a young girl at his concert could be said to betray the dwindling self-confidence of a fading star.

Voorsanger grew up in the same neighbourhood as one of the members of the American independ-ent band Codeine. The band's introspective and bleak lyrics ensured that they had a large cult following in the early '90s and they even shared a record label – Sub Pop – with Nirvana. In an inverse of the star/fan relationship, band member John Engle gave Voorsanger all the fan letters the band had received over a three-month period. The installation, *Codeine*, 1994, consists of the letters together with Voorsanger's correspondence with the band while their album *The White Birch*, 1994, plays in the background. The viewer is offered a rare insight into what it is like to be at the receiving end of this adoration and unrequited love. In one, a needy fan writes: 'Thank you for talking to me at the gig in Pensacola.' Another portrays a fan's unnerving and unquestioning dedication: 'You've really changed my life.' Emma Mahony

# Michael Wilkinson

Born Wallasey, 1965. Lives and works in Glasgow.

*Lightning Strikes Twice*, 2000
Acrylic on glass
30.5 x 30.5 x 1 cm
Courtesy The Modern Institute,
Glasgow

*Record Collection*, 2000
Acrylic on MDF
2 are 18.5 x 18.5 x 0.6 cm
4 are 26.1 x 26.1 x 0.6 cm
42 are 31.4 x 31.4 x 0.6 cm
Courtesy Aberdeen Art Gallery
and Museums

Recreating objects from the recent past, Michael Wilkinson interweaves references to art and popular culture. His work encourages personal and nostalgic reflection on the past and on the role youth and subcultures play in the way we define ourselves.

In *Kit* and *Heidi,* both 2000, Wilkinson takes two objects that have resonance for many of his generation, loose-weave canvas army surplus bags which were common in the Indie music scene in the late '80s and early '90s, rarely left unadorned, customised with paint or ballpoint pen with the names of friends or bands.

Likewise, Wilkinson's bags are lovingly painted, *Kit* with a geometric pattern sampled from the poster for a recent untitled record by Kit Clayton, another simply with the name Heidi. What this signifies remains ambiguous. Is Heidi a person or a band? Is it her bag or a sign of teenage infatuation? Perhaps the answers lie with our own experiences.

At about the same time music was changing. Vinyl records began to be replaced with CDs and acid house began to establish itself. Until then it was through 12 inch records that young people first attempted to define themselves, their musical tastes and personal possessions. The tactile qualities of vinyl, watching the needle pass across the surface and the hours spent examining in detail the cover artwork could never be recreated by diminutive CDs. Each disc became engrained with memories, the care and attention required by vinyl records added a further emotional investment in music.

In *Collection,* 2000, Wilkinson presents us with a facsimile of his record collection reproduced in paint on wood. Stripped of the textual and visual signifiers present in the original, each representation has been pared down to the abstract shapes and colours of its background. Presented in stacks as they would be in a record shop, Wilkinson tempts us to leaf through his possessions. Like the characters in Nick Hornby's novel *High Fidelity* whose whole lives are contained in their record collections, we are invited to reflect on our past by recognising personal moments within these abstracted cover designs. Chris Hammonds

# Stephen Willats

Born London, 1943. Lives and works in London.

*Model Dwellings*, Aug/Dec 1982
Photographic prints, acrylic paint,
Letraset text, ink, pencil,
objects on card
Two panels, each 90 x 144 cm
Courtesy the artist and
Victoria Miro Gallery, London

Stephen Willats's practice explores models for the creative transformation and 'self-organisation' of individuals within society. His interest in punk and the various subcultures associated with it, came directly off the back of his earlier work with the displaced communities resident in the tower blocks and housing estates which sprung up in West London in the '70s.

In 1981 Willats entered the 'world of the night'. It was a step which would prove to further his engagement with the DIY ethos of early '80s post-punk, a subculture which was perhaps more resourceful in its self-organisation than punk, its predecessor. Willats's so-called 'world of the night' centered on small spontaneously created clubs which were being fashioned by small communities or individuals who felt alienated from 'normal society' which they associated with the daytime. Held at regular clubs on quiet nights, the Cha Cha Club, located in an old railway arch under Charing Cross Station, was the most famous and perhaps the most inclusive. Others traded on their exclusivity. The Anarchy Centre was a meeting place for Mohicans; of all the clubs Willats frequented it was among the most disaffecting. As its title suggests, the Anarchy Centre promoted taboo dress codes and deviant behaviour, directives which were enforced by the clubs hostile atmosphere and very loud music.

Willats's engagement with this club culture lasted for five years during which time he made a series of works in collaboration with the club's members and organisers. *Model Dwellings*, Aug/Dec 1982, reflects his incursion into the attitudes, beliefs and day-to-day lives of the members of Model Dwellings, a pioneering electronic music club with a futuristic vision. The format the work takes is the result of the active participation of the club's members with the artist. The first of the work's two panels focuses on their individual identities and sensibilities and the latter represents their communal point of reference, the club itself and the sense of community it offers its members.

Emma Mahony

Questions/Answers

| | Why did you buy your first record? | What record made you change the way you look? | What's your favourite album cover? | What music do you claim as your own? | What record would you like to have played at your funeral? |
|---|---|---|---|---|---|
| **Maike Abetz & Oliver Drescher** | …it's all part of growing up…. | My Generation by The Who | And don't the kids just love it by Television Personalities, Computer Welt by Kraftwerk, The Psychedelic Sounds of the 13th Floor Elevators by 13th Floor Elevators | Mod, psychedelia, punk and Kraftwerk | Turn on – Tune in – Drop out by Dr Timothy Leary |
| **Dave Allen** | I had some money, it was burning a hole in my pocket | ? | Frampton Comes Alive/Live and Dangerous by Thin Lizzy also the White Album by The Beatles | Whatever I'm listening to. Anything I've bought or taped. Whatever I've heard or read about and would like to hear | ? |
| **Luke Caulfield** | Excess testosterone | X-Ray Spex | Paranoid by Black Sabbath | tseirP saduJ | It could have been a brilliant career by Belle and Sebastian |
| **Sean Dower** | I was coerced by my brothers, who had already spent all their own pocket money on records and considered my pocket money an untapped resource | Looking Through Gary Gilmore's Eyes by The Adverts | Sergeant Pepper's as adapted by Christian Marclay, Autobahn by Kraftwerk, Limited Edition by Can | The music that I make myself | Anything by Conlan Nancarrow, a live, acoustic version of What will death be like? by Momus and Here Comes the Bride, as the coffin is engulfed by the flames |
| **Sam Durant** | My friend Danny told me to buy it. The record was the Jimi Hendrix film soundtrack. He later convinced me to trade it to him for Deep Purple's Made in Japan | Minor Threat's first 45 and SS Decontrol's first record, I think it had a black cover | Impossible to answer | I'm not sure I understand the question. Unfortunately, I played in several bands so I guess I have to take responsibility for that | The first Black Sabbath record, backwards of course |
| **Douglas Gordon** | I have no idea. The more challenging question for me is – why did I buy my last record? | The first album by The Smiths | White Album by The Beatles | Whatever goes in through my ears and stays in my head | Whatever the people want to hear, maybe a juke box could be a good compromise |
| **Peter Harris** | In 1975 I bought a Chuck Berry album because my friend had one of his songs that I liked | Never Mind the Bollocks by The Sex Pistols | The David Bowie bootleg Midnight in Vancouver | The ones I wrote | I'll not be a stranger, the folk spiritual song by Bob Dylan from the Hard to Find Vol.7 bootleg music from The Law Hideout |
| **Paul Housley** | It was the Red Album by The Beatles on cassette. I needed and wanted it in equal measure | Any number of records between the ages of 10 and 22 | This changes daily depending on my mood – anything from The Beatles for Sale to Wow by Moby Grape, with a special mention for Bummed by The Happy Mondays | I wouldn't claim any music as my own | This would be a compilation tape which would be given away to anyone that came, to be played at their own leisure |
| **Scott King** | My dad bought me my first record, Far Far Away by Slade. For some reason I cried. I think I was so happy. It's still a favourite today | Quadrophenia by The Who, I Just Can't Stop It by The Beat (I was 10) | The Beatles' White Album designed by Richard Hamilton and Joy Division's Unknown Pleasures designed by Peter Saville | Earl Brutus | You Doo Right by Can |

| | Why did you buy your first record? | What record made you change the way you look? | What's your favourite album cover? | What music do you claim as your own? | What record would you like to have played at your funeral? |
|---|---|---|---|---|---|
| **Christian Marclay** | Because I was in love with the girl on the cover | None, but maybe looking at Jean Tinguely's machines made me change the way I hear | The Beatles' *White album* designed by Richard Hamilton | All music that enters my ears becomes mine | *4'3"* by John Cage |
| **Paul McDevitt** | I got so excited by the teaser poster campaign for *Ghostbusters* that I bought the Ray Parker Junior single | Dinosaur Jr., Sonic Youth, Public Enemy, but mainly Jane's Addiction | *Eureka* by Jim O'Rourke | No one else I know has any albums by Oingo Boingo | *No Diggity* by Blackstreet (featuring Dr. Dre) |
| **Jonathan Monk** | It was on sale | *Baggy Trousers* by Madness | Second-hand copies (soiled) of The Beatles' *White Album* | My mother cleaning my father's piano | *There is a light that never goes out* by The Smiths |
| **Dave Muller** | It was *Snoopy Vs. The Red Baron* by the Royal Guardsmen. I bought it at a garage sale down the street from my house when I was eight. I think I got that and a Beau Brummel's record for 25 cents. I bought it because a friend of mine had it when we were five and I remembered it | An early Big Black ep. I think it was called *Bulldozer* | *Good Morning Mr. Walker* by Joseph Spence or *Crazy! Baby* by Jimmy Smith | Things I've written | The last of the *26 Madrigals: Rounds and Canons* by Moondog. You can find it as track 35 on *Moondog* |
| **Seamus Nicolson** | The first record I bought was *Destroyer* by Kiss. I was probably about ten years old at the time, so the band's cartoon hero image appealed to me | There wasn't one record in particular that changed the way I looked. It was more to do with a particular experience in which music played a major role that changed my appearance. After the techno trance raves that I went to in the summer of '95 I changed from someone who looked relatively normal into a longhaired, combat trousered, baggy psychedelic jumper wearer | *Surfer Rosa* by The Pixies | Any music with which I associate memories of formative years or happy experiences. Bands such as Joy Division, Sonic Youth, Pixies, Pavement, Mercury Rev as well as more mainstream groups like New Order and Cure. I would have to include some oldies as well – The Beatles, The Velvet Underground, Neil Young and early David Bowie. It's impossible to narrow it down | Any record by King Tubby |
| **James Pyman** | The drawing of the fly on the label frightened and excited me | Wagner | *Dub Housing* by Pere Ubu | Outlaw Country (Waylon, Willie, etc.) | *Native New Yorker* by Odyssey |
| **George Shaw** | Because, as always, I misunderstood the world | What record didn't! *The Specials* by The Specials | *Searching for the Young Soul Rebels* by Dexy's Midnight Runners | Like most people of my age I suffer from the open wound of being ever too slightly young for punk. So it has to be 2 Tone | *Enjoy Yourself* by The Specials |
| **Ross Sinclair** | I thought Gary Glitter was incredibly cool and I wanted to be in his gang – how wrong can you be? | X-Ray Spex, first album, *Never Mind the Bollocks* by The Sex Pistols and the first Clash/ Stranglers – the whole punk thing really, but 2 years too late, in '79 (I was only 13) | The one I made for the first Soup Dragons album – it was so exciting to make any records then, especially an album – the cover was a picture of a big flashing star construction I made which said on it 'This is our Art … Useless, Boring, Impotent, Elitist and very very Beautiful'. I think it summed us up nicely, though I probably should have added the word pretentious as well | It's the first song you play in the morning and it's the last one you play before you go out at night. Other people might say they don't understand it but if sure as hell makes sense to you. It's the tune you play majestically, top volume, at 3am, and fuck the neighbours. The passion of this music makes life worth living. And the power of the music will make you wonder if art could ever be as good | *Everything Flows* by Teenage Fanclub but played live b∞ Norman Blake on an old acoustic guitar |

| Name | | | | | |
|---|---|---|---|---|---|
| **Bob & Roberta Smith** | Because I liked both Johnny Morris and Thomas the Tank Engine | I once melted a record and made a hat but I can't remember whom it was by | Help by The Beatles | My music | 4 minutes of silence by John Cage |
| **Frances Stark** | So I could listen to it over and over and not have to wait for it to come on the radio | X Los Angeles, Jealous Again by Black Flag | Still by Joy Division | California punk & Killing Joke/Siouxsie type post-punk 1980–84 | You're supposed to play records at funerals? |
| **John Strutton** | Because it had swear words on it | Are Friends Electric by Tubeway Army | Honey by The Ohio Players | The soundtrack to Grease and Jilted John by Jilted John | The Laughing Policeman by Charles Penrose |
| **Jessica Voorsanger** | I liked it. I wanted to live the disco freedom of the Love Rollercoaster (I was 10 years old) | A Hard Day's Night by The Beatles | Up to Date by The Partridge Family | Bubble gum. It makes me happy and sticks in my head like glue and won't go away | Hall of Fame by Georgie Fame |
| **Michael Wilkinson** | Mike Post | None have really. I am a cider drinker by the Wurzels may have been responsible for me avoiding looking like a village idiot though. How successfully is another matter | Low and Lust For Life are always favourites | All of it | Wish you were here by Pink Floyd |
| **Stephen Willats** | Because I thought the local record shop was a groovy place to hang out | Blue Suede Shoes, because I have worn blue suede shoes ever since | Low Flying Aircraft, a model of an aircraft which moves across the face of the disc on wire, all handmade by the band | West London R & B | None |
| **Elisabetta Fabrizi**<br>Exhibitions Organiser | Shock the Monkey by Peter Gabriel when I was 8. I loved to dance to the rhythm and wanted to listen to it all the time so I bought it | Psycho Candy by Jesus and Mary Chain | Plastic Surgery Disasters by Dead Kennedys | Fugazi. No Means No. Nick Cave | Einsturzende Neubauten, Blume (English version song by Anita Lane from Tabula Rasa, 1993) |
| **Emma Mahony**<br>Curator | Brothers in Arms by Dire Straits when I was 10 because I loved Why Worry | Albums by Pearl Jam and Stiff Little Fingers | The Velvet Underground & Nico by The Velvet Underground | Anything by U2, Thin Lizzy, Madonna | Dancing in the Moon Light by Thin Lizzy |
| **Stephen Snoddy**<br>Director | Because my older brothers and sister had records and I hadn't any yet | The Bay City Rollers (unfortunately!) | Power, Corruption and Lies by New Order | Anything by The Undertones or Stiff Little Fingers | Heaven Knows I am Miserable Now by The Smiths |
| **Peter B. Willberg**<br>Designer | Santana Greatest Hits because I loved the cover | Slowhand by Eric Clapton | Wheels of Fire by Cream | 44 Duets for Violin by Béla Bartók Johannes Passion by J.S. Bach | Haydn String Quartets |
| **Mark Wilsher**<br>Writer | Childish desire to collect all the number one singles | Bitches Brew by Miles Davis | There Is No One That Will Take Care Of You by Palace Brothers | Easy by Faith Over Reason | None. I would like silence |

Catalogue published on the occasion of *Air Guitar: Art Reconsidering Rock Music*, curated by Emma Mahony

'Air Guitar: Art Reconsidering Rock Music' is an exhibition organised by Milton Keynes Gallery and touring to Cornerhouse, Manchester, Angel Row, Nottingham and Tullie House, Carlisle, funded by the National Touring Programme through the Arts Council of England.

**Milton Keynes Gallery**
12 July – 1 September 2002

**Cornerhouse, Manchester**
21 September – 3 November 2002

**Angel Row, Nottingham**
11 January – 1 March 2003

**Tullie House, Carlisle**
22 March – 18 May 2003

Catalogue published by Milton Keynes Gallery
© 2002, Milton Keynes Gallery and the authors

ISBN 0-9536755-7-2

Edited by Stephen Snoddy and Elisabetta Fabrizi
Design Peter B. Willberg and Nanni Goebel
at Clarendon Road Studio
Printed by Specialblue Ltd.
Edition 2000

Milton Keynes Gallery
900 Midsummer Boulevard
Central Milton Keynes
MK9 3QA
England
Tel  +44 (0) 1908 676 900
Fax +44 (0) 1908 558 308
Email mkgallery@mktgc.co.uk
Website www.mkweb.co.uk/mkg

Director Stephen Snoddy
Exhibitions Organiser Elisabetta Fabrizi
Head of Press & Marketing Katharine Sorensen
Marketing & Development Assistant Emma Dummett
Development Co-ordinator Ronny Kimbell
Education Co-ordinator Kirsten Gibbs
Education Assistant Victoria Mayes
Gallery Co-ordinator Lee Farmer
Gallery Technician Emma Gregory
Gallery Assistants Kelly Blyth, Lorna Gemmell,
Nick Horrigan, Emma Wilde

With special thanks to all the artists,
their galleries and the lenders

The curator wishes to thank:
Stuart Comer
Eileen Daly
Adrienne Deery
Ellen Devereux
Elisabetta Fabrizi
Nanni Goebel
Chris Hammonds
Teresa Gleadowe
Niamh Ann Kelly
T. A. W. Mahony
Duncan McLaren
Emily Pethick
Lis Rackham
Stephen Snoddy
Peter B. Willberg
Mark Wilshire

**Revenue Funding**
MK G gratefully acknowledges financial support
from Southern Arts, Milton Keynes Council and
English Partnerships.

Front cover:
Scott King
*The Rolling Stones, 12 September 1969, Altamont
Raceway, Livermore, USA,* 1999
Inkjet print
102 x 152 cm
Courtesy Magnani, London

Back cover:
Scott King
*The Who, 18 August 1974, Charlton Athletic Football
Ground, London, England,* 1999
Inkjet print
102 x 152 cm
Courtesy Magnani, London